NORA EPHRON
THE LAST INTERVIEW
and OTHER CONVERSATIONS

MELVILLE HOUSE
BROOKLYN · LONDON

NORA EPHRON: THE LAST INTERVIEW
AND OTHER CONVERSATIONS

"Nice to See Nora Ephron Happy in Her Work" © 1974 by Michael S. Lasky.
First published in *Writer's Digest* in April, 1974.

"Feminist with a Funny Bone" © 2007 by Patrick McGilligan. First published
in *Backstory 5: Interviews with Screenwriters of the 1990s*.

"'I Remember Nothing': Nora Ephron on Life, Death, and Hot Dogs" first
appeared in Salon.com. An online version remains in the
Salon archives. Reprinted with permission.

"The Last Interview" © 2012 by Kathryn Borel. First published in
The Believer magazine in March 2012.

First Melville House printing: December 2015

Melville House Publishing   8 Blackstock Mews
46 John Street   and   Islington
Brooklyn, NY 11201   London N4 2BT

mhpbooks.com   facebook.com/mhpbooks   @melvillehouse

Library of Congress Cataloging-in-Publication Data
Ephron, Nora.
    Nora Ephron : the last interview and other conversations.
    Brooklyn, NY : Melville House, [2015]
    The last interview series
    LCCN 2015039514
    ISBN 978-1-61219-524-7 (paperback)
    ISBN 978-161219-525-4 (ebook)
    LCSH: Ephron, Nora—Interviews. | BISAC: BIOGRAPHY &
AUTOBIOGRAPHY / Entertainment & Performing Arts. | BIOGRAPHY
& AUTOBIOGRAPHY / Literary. | LITERARY COLLECTIONS /
American / General.
    LCC PS3555.P5 Z46 2015 | DDC 814/.54—dc23
    LC record available at http://lccn.loc.gov/2015039514

Printed in the United States of America
10 9 8 7 6 5 4 3 2 1

NORA EPHRON

CONTENTS

NICE TO SEE NORA EPHRON HAPPY IN HER WORK

INTERVIEW BY MICHAEL S. LASKY
WRITER'S DIGEST
APRIL 1974

At thirty-two, Nora Ephron is everywhere and it didn't take her very long to get there. To interview her for even just a few hours can be nearly as impossible as typing with your elbows.

Nora is elusive these days. If she isn't in California or in Houston, covering Bobby Riggs's tennis matches for Esquire, New York, *or* Oui, *then she is off to France for a one-week spree of the best Michelin three-star restaurants—all expenses paid. Then again, if she isn't in France or California or in her sparsely furnished New York apartment, she is probably in Israel covering the Mideast turmoil, or in Las Vegas for the fun of it.*

She began her rise to journalistic success fresh out of college as a copy girl and articles clipper at Newsweek, *which she says was "the worst job in the world and I was actually good at it." She moved quickly and assuredly, though, onto writing features for the* New York Post *and then as a full-time freelancer.*

In 1970, Viking Press published a collection of her felicitous writing under the apt title, Wallflower at the Orgy. *At the time, writer Rex Reed readily noted that her writing was "great chunky spoonfuls served in tasty style by a fresh, inventive observer who stalks the phonies and cherubs alike, sniffing them out like a hungry tiger, clamping her pretty teeth down in all the spots where it hurts the most, then leaving all her victims better off than they were before they met Nora Ephron."*

In recent years, Nora has been a lively columnist and writer for Esquire *but presently works in the same capacity for* New York *magazine, which "made her an offer she couldn't refuse." (Her column at both magazines has gone under the same name: simply, "Women.")*

I interviewed Nora Ephron on one of the rare days when she was at home with her cat in her New York Midtown apartment that overlooks the Ziegfield Theatre, a porno moviehouse, and a Chinese restaurant. She wedged me between some morning activities and a late-afternoon appointment at the beauty parlor, where she "gets to catch up on all the women's magazines."

As we headed down the noisy New York streets at the end of the interview, she described herself at my request: "I am skinny and have a long face, long chin, and dark hair and a snaggletooth that I've worked very hard to get. My hair droops over my left eye so no one will notice that my left eyelid droops."

Now that you have some idea of what she looks like, we can find out what she has to say.

LASKY: How did you get started in freelance writing?

EPHRON: I was a reporter at the *New York Post* for about three years where I had been producing feature stories. I got a call from Helen Gurley Brown. She had just started working at *Cosmopolitan* and needed stories written quickly, for which news reporters have a reputation. I did a crappy little piece for her on the life of a Copacabana showgirl—that was my first real freelance money. I had tried to get articles printed before, though, but they were all rejected. This was before

I had even started working at the *Post*. Some of these were rudely rejected, I might add.

LASKY: What do you mean, *rudely*?

EPHRON: One article I had submitted to *Glamour* was returned with a note that just about said never submit anything to us again . . . it will be fine if we never *hear* from you again. I think you could call that rude. But to go on, as I continued my work at the *Post* over the years, I met people and my byline became familiar, so I got some freelance offers like *Cosmo*, *The New York Times Book Review*. And when I left the *Post* to freelance full-time . . .

LASKY: What prompted you to do that?

EPHRON: Well, there were two things. For one, I wasn't really growing as a writer . . . I got as much from newspaper writing as I thought I could. Another thing was I had gotten married. Being married to someone who made a certain amount of money meant that I could take the gamble on my first year as a freelance writer. If I didn't make as much as I did when I was a reporter, there was someone who was going to take up the slack. I was pretty sure that I could make that $10,000 figure, and I just about did. As a matter of fact, until this year I never made more than that.

LASKY: How much money can you or do you make, now that you are a full-time freelancer on your own? Do you reach a necessity threshold or one for a style of living that you were used to?

EPHRON: Both. There is the necessity threshold and then there is the Henri Bendel threshold. If you don't write books I don't really see making more than $25,000, and I think that is rough-going to make even *that*. Most of my women friends who do it make somewhere in the $15–$18,000 bracket and that includes doing a certain amount of hooking. Prostituting yourself . . . writing for *Woman's Day* and supermarket-type magazines. I say "hooking" because these women realize they are writing under their level. I just think that there are free subjects that I want to cover that I could handle at the level *Woman's Day* would want. That would mean a certain amount of compromise and oversimplification involved in the writing of it. I'll give you an example.

The other day I got a call from the editors of *McCall's* asking me if I wanted to write a story about Dorothy Day. He said the catch was that I would have to spend the first few pages explaining who Dorothy Day was to the readers. I said, "What a shame!" But still, to be given a chance to write about the woman to eight million readers who might never have heard of her tends to make me want to do the piece anyway. But I won't be able to do it at the intellectual level that is the most rewarding to me as a writer.

LASKY: Did your being a writer have anything to do with the way you met your husband?

EPHRON: I was working on a diet series at the *Post* and putting quotes from books at the top of each article. I had used a quote from Bruce Jay Friedman's *Stern*, which is indirectly about a fat person, and I had seen *How to Be a Jewish Mother* and I knew it had something about food in it. On the back of the book was this picture of the person who had written it, Dan Greenburg, and it said that he was single. And it said that he had written for *Monocle* magazine.

Now *Monocle* was this periodical of satire, which its editor always called the "sporadical," because it came out so infrequently. *Monocle* was edited by a close friend, Victor Navasky, who really got me my job at the *New York Post*. In 1962, when the New York newspaper strike was on, *Monocle* put out parodies of each paper and I had done the parody of the Leonard Lyons column, which appeared in the *Post*. The editors of the *Post* were livid and wanted to sue. But Dorothy Schiff, the publisher, said, "Don't be fools, *hire* them. They can write for the *Post* if they can parody it."

Well, anyway, here on the back of this book it said that this funny, single person had worked for *Monocle*. So I called Victor and said, "What about Dan Greenburg?" and he knew exactly what I meant. But he told me that he was going with someone and it took a year before Dan disentangled himself. Victor and his wife planned a dinner party where we could meet. And then we got married and now we are separated. Now how's *that* for a really beautiful story?

LASKY: What type of work were you doing at the *Post*?

EPHRON: I was doing features . . . what I called *froth* . . . a lot of profiles of show-business people, Luci and Lynda Bird

Johnson and their weddings, and I did a certain amount of sob-sister stuff and a few series on Johnny Carson, dieting and the like. And I liked it. I never felt that I wanted to write about something "serious."

LASKY: Writers who want to, but haven't, written for top magazines such as *McCall's* and *Esquire*, and nonwriting readers, think that writers such as yourself have glamorous lives. Do you agree?

EPHRON: Oh, sure. Look—I have just gotten back to New York from ten days at the Beverly Hills Hotel, where I was doing a piece on Bobby Riggs, and there is no way not to think that you don't have a glamorous life after ten days there on an expense account. It is so glorious and actually the only way to stay there, because every time you go to get your car, it costs you $250 in tips. Freelance writing gives you the opportunity to travel—particularly in the last year I have done a lot more of that—I went to the Democratic Convention; I went to the first Bobby Riggs match. And it *is* wonderful.

There are an awful lot of people you get to spend time with that you wouldn't otherwise and as many events that you feel fortunate to have seen. I think that readers believe that the writer becomes friends with the people he interviews and writes about—and I think there *are* some writers who do that—but that hasn't happened to me. I do think it is dangerous because then you write the article to please them, which is a terrible error. So it isn't glamorous in that you get to *befriend* all those people. You are not really part of their lives.

Listen, in two weeks I am going on a junket—a disgusting and unethical thing, right?

LASKY: Right.

EPHRON: This liquor company invited twelve journalists to spend one week flying around France in Lear Jets to the three-star Michelin restaurants. I mean this is absurd; really tell people about this. You know, I am jealous of *myself*! Now if I was going to write about it—but I am not, I don't plan to write a word about it—but if I was, I would call a magazine and ask them to pay the expenses for a clear conscience. But one of the nicest things about the trip is not having to write anything. I mean I went to Africa recently and it was such a pleasure to just go and not have to use it for some story. To go just for the experience.

LASKY: Moving away from this glamorous and decadent life of yours for a minute, can you say something about *how* you work, what your routine is?

EPHRON: I don't *have* much of a routine. I go through periods where I work a great deal at all hours of the day whenever I am around the typewriter, and then I go through spells where I don't do anything. I just sort of have lunch—*all day*. I never have been able to stick to a schedule. I work when there is something due or when I am really excited about a piece.

I have to produce one column a month. My contract with New York calls for one per month plus five long pieces a year. That's all I have to do. And if I did just the columns I could more or less scrape by.

When I am in a maniacal work period I don't stop doing other things, you know. I usually don't work more than four hours per day, which is usually over the day mixed in with talking on the phone, listening to records, and smoking cigarettes. So the amount of time I spend actually *writing* is quite small.

Someone once told me a story about a man who was an editor for *Playboy*. He got some sort of chronometer that he attached to his typewriter. He used to write all day long, and he called this person I know and said he had been clocking himself and he was spending forty-three minutes a day at the typewriter and that's why he put this thing on it. So he would really sit there and force himself to work. And a week later he shot himself. Of course, this is not to say that this is why he killed himself. Still, it's something to think about.

LASKY: What happens when you can't get a piece started, when you are completely cold?

EPHRON: I am never *completely* cold. I don't have writer's block, really. I do have times when I can't get the lead and that is the only part of the story that I have serious trouble with. I don't write a *word* of the article until I have the lead. It just sets the whole tone—the whole point of view. I know exactly where I am going as soon as I have the lead. That can take me three or four days and sometimes a week. But as for being cold—as a newspaper reporter you learn that no one tolerates you if you are cold; it's one thing you are not allowed to be. It's not professional. You have to turn the story in. There is no room for the artist.

And so trouble with the lead is as close as I get to being cold, and yes, I do go away from it for a while and go buy a pair of shoes or have dinner. And I know that maybe if I can talk to someone at dinner I'll find the thing I am looking for.

LASKY: Do you have any distractions that particularly bother you?

EPHRON: Life. I mean the main thing that distracts me is the pressure to go on with one's life. That you have to stop to have lunch with someone or you have to take the cat to the vet . . . just the everyday routine is what bothers me. I mean things like the supermarket. I have been to the supermarket maybe twice in five months. I just can't seem to get there.

Being single is a distraction. I mean one of the things about marriage that is good for both men and women is that it frees you from all that energy that you use to put into dating. You can put it into work. You don't have to worry about who is going to take you to the dinner party tomorrow. It takes time to be single, it seems to me.

LASKY: Once you have all the notes and you are ready for writing, what comes the hardest?

EPHRON: As I said before, the lead. It carries the point of the story, as I said. I have this great story about leads that I always tell. I had this fantastic high school journalism teacher who left the teaching business almost instantly and is now some sort of millionaire record-store owner in Los Angeles. Anyway, the first day in the class we were learning to write leads. So he dictated this set of facts: "The principal of Beverly Hills High School announced today that the faculty will travel to Fresno on Thursday for a seminar on the new mathematics. Speaking there will be Edward Teller, Albert Einstein, and . . . oh, Margaret Mead." So we all sat and wrote these leads that sounded almost exactly like what I just said. And we turned them in and he stood up and said, "The lead to this story is 'There will be no school Thursday.'" There was moment of the lightbulb going off in your head and I thought to myself, "Ohmigod, it's about the point!" Ever since then I am always sure that I am *missing* the point.

LASKY: Did you ever really miss the point?

EPHRON: God, yes. When I was living in Paris in 1963 and freelancing for *The New York Times* Overseas Edition, I went to do a story on how they were cleaning Notre Dame—they were cleaning all the buildings in France to get them from a gray to a beautiful creamy color. I didn't speak French well at all and did these terrible interviews in pigeon French. After I turned in the piece, my editor called me and said, "The piece is fine but you are going to die when you see what you left out." I got this sinking feeling in my stomach and I asked, "What did I leave out?" And he said, "The reason they are cleaning Notre Dame is it is its four hundredth birthday." I felt so foolish. I had no idea.

LASKY: Once you get a go-ahead on an idea for an article, do you have an outline to organize your material?

EPHRON: No. I just seem to muddle through. I interview people and they tell me about other people to interview. I talk to many more people than I ever quote. And I know in my mind what I have to cover. I spend much *too* much time researching things. But I think you have to know too much so you can be on top of your subject.

LASKY: Is humor essential to a story? Every piece of yours always seems to have its share of humor.

EPHRON: Well, it's just that my point of view happens to be faintly cynical or humorous—and that's just the way I see things and that's how it comes out when I write it. It is not anything I am conscious of, though. A piece about a "heavy" subject can be written a little bit light so the piece doesn't seem quite as heavy. You've mainly got to trust yourself to write the way *you* feel about something.

LASKY: When do you use direct and indirect quotes?

EPHRON: I try to use direct quotes when a quote captures the personality of the person who said it or if it would take me twice as long to say the same thing paraphrasing it. I can't stand writers who quote people saying very mundane lines like, "I was born in 1934." You read something like that and wonder to yourself why did he quote *that*, it doesn't take you anywhere, or show you anything that the writer couldn't have done himself in a more interesting way. I don't like to use long stretches of direct quotes either because I think they should be broken up.

LASKY: Do you use a tape recorder for your interviews?

EPHRON: Yes. From time to time. Generally, though, I think that there are very few people worth listening to twice. For the main subject of profiles I will use one, but I have this type of speedwriting that works as well for most interviews. I will go over what I wrote in the notebook and fill in the gaps after the interview . . . words that I might have missed. Besides, I can't stand to transcribe.

LASKY: Will you let the interviewees read the manuscript or their quotes for approval?

EPHRON: Well, that is one "trick" that might work for some writers. I have tried other tricks like writing with different colored paper in the hopes that it will make me write better. I'll switch colors of paper in the middle of a story and I will go through *The Paris Review* interviews hoping to find the secret of how to write a novel in six weeks, but of course you don't.

LASKY: How long does it take you to write a story?

EPHRON: My column takes anywhere from two days to a week, and longer articles take three days sometimes, and then again, sometimes they take two months. The story on feminine deodorant sprays [*Esquire*, March 1973], took me a year because I worked on it off and on. It was just a killer. I didn't have to *take* that long at it, but that's the way I worked it.

LASKY: How many times will you write a story before you hand it in?

EPHRON: The way I write is that I keep writing over and over again. What will happen is I will write the first three pages and I'll have to get this transition that stumps me, and rather than think too hard about it, I will *retype* the first three pages in the hopes that the speed of my typing will leap me over this transition. And if it doesn't, I will begin again. And what results is that the beginnings of my pieces are always better written than the ends of them. A piece that I turn in is probably in its twelfth draft—every section has been through the typewriter many times. I usually think an article is finished when the last time I go through it I don't change more than a word a page. So you see I don't write the conventional first draft and then second. By the time I get to the last page, the whole work is almost in final draft except for the end.

LASKY: Are you conscious of different types of styles that you will use for different magazines?

EPHRON: Yeah. Since I have been lucky enough during the last few years to have the choice of where I want to write, I try to pick the magazines that best suit my *natural* style—*Esquire* and *New York*, for example. I do find that when I reread what I have written for *The New York Times Magazine* that I edited myself a little bit too much—that I cut out anything that *they* might think is flashy—I flatten it out because I think of the *Times* as a place where the writing isn't terribly interesting. And of course on the women's magazines; you know you find that you tend to simplify and be a little girlish and coquettish. I must say that I have not done anything for *Ms.* But I have some friends who have and they report that the problem there is the exact opposite. I try to stay away from places where I sense tension between the magazine's point of view and my own.

LASKY: Don't you think it is a bit presumptuous for a writer to write a piece thinking that readers are going to care what your opinion was before or after you started the article?

EPHRON: I see your point and that's why it'd better be interesting. You better *make* them care about what you think. It had better be quirky or perverse or thoughtful enough so that you hit some chord in them. Otherwise, it doesn't work. I mean, we've all read pieces where we thought, "Oh, who gives a damn."

LASKY: What was there about the articles you had written that made it possible to put them together into an anthology other than the good reason of its title, *Wallflower at the Orgy*?

EPHRON: Well, there was nothing that made it possible to put it together except that I wanted to have them published. And I had a contract with Viking on another book that they wanted very much, so to appease me they put *Wallflower* out—but then I was terrible and naughty and never completed the other book.

LASKY: Do you use a thesaurus?

EPHRON: I don't have one.

LASKY: Well, aren't you like most writers who don't have a particular word they want at their command at the time they need it? What do you do? Is it just that you have a large command of vocabulary?

EPHRON: No, I think I have a very small command. I think all my articles could be put out as *Dr. Seuss* books that use thirty words or less. I don't use words that are complicated. For example, I was reading a Doris Lessing book on Africa and she kept talking about jacaranda trees. Now I have no idea what kind of tree that is—I would much rather she said trees with purple and yellow blossoms or whatever the hell it is. The name doesn't mean anything to me. I don't have a whole lot of trouble finding words because I use fairly simple ones over and over again. I use the word "clear" repeatedly—too much. Like: "It seems clear that . . . " It is horrifying how many times I use it.

LASKY: What are some of the problems of being a woman freelancer?

EPHRON: Well, I think that there are certain magazines that will just not assign pieces to women or even think of women in connection with certain subjects such as economics or politics. I'm involved with a group of women writers who have an action against the Sunday *New York Times*. Statistics for the magazine section are just *shocking*. I mean year in and year out, 12 percent of their writers are women, and then only for certain subjects. And there are plenty of women who could write better stuff than the awful things they publish.

That's the only serious problem I can think of and it is serious because it's about making a living. But on the other hand, there are some distinct advantages. For example, many women are married and have the luxury of being freelance writers. It just doesn't pay that much and if you are in a two-income household it works out better for you. I am now in a one-income household and for the first time I have had to think about making a living from full-time freelance writing which is *very, very* difficult, unless you write books. So for an *un*married woman freelance writer it is no more difficult in *one* sense than for a man, because it is a very low-paying profession. The rates have not gone up. When I left the newspaper business I was making $10,000, and if I stayed I would be up to $16–$17,000, which is 60 percent more. The freelance rates have not gone up 60 or 70 percent in that five-year period. The top prices are pretty much the same; the *bottom* prices are pretty much the same. There are very few places that have lifted their rates with the rise in the standard of living.

LASKY: Do you think it is easier for a woman because people will open up more to her than to a man?

EPHRON: Not really. I know that there are certain types of people who just don't take women seriously at all. I think that policemen, detectives, athletes, all of your basic locker-room-boy professions are very difficult to get in contact with. They have never talked with a woman before so why are they going to start now!

Businessmen are a *little* easier but not *much* . . . Politicians are also rough. There are some women writers who think subjects do open up more to women but I don't. And some who think that you can flirt with the men you interview and will do it. I don't know. I flirt with only about two men a year—never on the job. I have been pleasant. Charming, even . . . I hope. My tendency is to believe that it just about balances out with your skill. Interview subjects do tend to underrate women interviewers, and it seems to me the best approach to this is not to be helpless and feminine but to work terribly hard at the beginning to prove yourself, to show them that you *know* what you are talking about—that you've read up and that you are not there cold.

LASKY: Nora, you became an editor yourself when you edited that *Esquire* issue on women [July 1973]. How did you find yourself as an editor?

EPHRON: I think I was a terrible editor. There were two problems . . . One was that if the idea for the article had been mine and was assigned to someone else, I was invariably disappointed in the finished piece because I would have written it differently. I don't think you can be a really good editor while hanging on to a writer's ego. The second problem was: because I am a writer, I was absolutely hopeless when it came time to tell people to make changes. I would say: "I would like it if you do this, but don't feel you *have* to" . . . or "If you don't agree with it, don't do it—it's okay." I was too much the writer myself. I just couldn't bring myself to tell them what to do; too much in sympathy with them. I knew how they would feel having three words cut here and more there.

LASKY: Did you personally ever have that type of problem—where the editors would cut or change your piece without telling you?

EPHRON: Yes, *Cosmo* did that all the time. They would cut and change things and not send me galleys. *McCall's* cut a piece of mine without even a phone call.

I did a memoir *McCall's* bought. They published it peculiarly as "fiction"—because they don't have a category called "memoir." The next thing, I got the issue—actually I had to buy it. And I saw that they had made cuts. And I called the editor and asked, "Why didn't you tell me you were cutting the piece?" And she said, "It was a last-minute thing and we didn't really have time." I said, "Why couldn't you have called me or my answering service and said, 'You have an hour to get back to us, we have to cut a page and a half.' Why didn't you give me the option of finding the places to cut?" I was really furious—livid. And I wrote a nasty letter to the editor about it. Editors tend to treat writers exactly the way directors treat actors, which is as these hopeless children who aren't professional enough to deal with things like that. I mean I rarely scream and yell, but all I want is the opportunity for me to make the changes they want. I was furious and the next time I got an assignment from them I said I wouldn't do it unless they promised to send me galleys and consult me for changes and cuts, which they did the next time.

LASKY: What advice would you give to writers who are just starting out or who would have been in the field for just a little while?

EPHRON: First of all, whatever you do, work in a field that has something to do with writing and publishing. So you will be exposed to what people are writing about and how they are writing, and, as important, so you will be exposed to people in the business who will get to know you and will call on you if they are looking for someone for a job. Secondly, you have to write. And if you don't have a job doing it, then you have to sit at home doing it. Of course, I don't see how a writer who wants to crack into national magazines and continue to write for them can do it living outside of New York or Los Angeles. It seems to me that your chances are much more difficult if you don't live in these cities. The main thing, though, is just to try and get published. If you are going to submit articles cold, chances are they won't be sold quickly, but they do get purchased that way. My erstwhile husband sold his first piece to *Esquire* when he was eighteen. You know he had 100 consecutive rejections after that but he *did* sell that first piece. But if you are going to send it in that way, by all means send it to the *managing* editor by name. Look on the masthead. Don't be dumb enough to send it to the top editor. Managing editors at most magazines seem to be the ones that route these things. I wish I could be more explicit but I never had much experience selling cold. I was on a panel recently and someone asked how you write a query letter. I don't really know. When I was at *Esquire* I know that there were a couple of query letters that came through that were clever enough so that the editors gave them assignments on spec . . . They would have been full assignments if the writers had had some published writing to show. So the main thing is to *get in print.*

LASKY: The old question: Does an agent help?

EPHRON: I never think so. I always think that agents can't help you when you need them and when you don't need them they are full of ways to help you. But I couldn't *live* without my agent. My agent couldn't help in my first years as a freelancer because I was hardly the writer that editors wanted to assign. Occasionally she would set up meetings for me with editors, which were always disastrous. I don't think editors are terribly courageous about assigning new writers, even though they say they are always looking for them. Agents don't really want to take on freelancers who are just starting out because it simply does not pay. Ten percent of a freelance writer's salary is nothing. They want the big book deals. Once you start selling you can not only *get* an agent but you really *need* one because those editors will screw you blind. I know from that three-month period I worked with writers as an editor at *Esquire.* We always gave more to writers who had agents. The agents *knew* what the going price was and there was no getting around them.

LASKY: What was the reaction to your story about your breasts that ran in *Esquire*? [Reprinted in the October 1973 issue.]

EPHRON: Well, I got a lot of mail; some of it was in the yeah-right-on vein, some of it was wonderfully perceptive. It was the most mail I have ever gotten about anything—about two hundred letters.

You know, I was very nervous about this piece. When I gave it to *Esquire* I told them I would not sell it if they put an illustration with it. I wanted it to be absolutely clear that it was *I* that was poking fun at myself, not them. So I had to make that stipulation because that art department wanted to do a picture of something like two maraschino cherries. I was very worried that people would think it was tasteless and how-far-is-this-confession-bit-going-to-go? In fact, I got a couple of letters that compared the article to Merle Miller's coming-out-of-the-closet piece he wrote for the *Times*—and that made me sad.

LASKY: What was some of the feedback you got from other pieces?

EPHRON: I got some, not ever much, mail about the piece I wrote on Henry Kissinger for *McCall's*. The point of that was while there wasn't much, what there was was dumb. Feedback varies in quality and quantity, from magazine to magazine. I don't think I ever got one letter for all the work I did for *Cosmopolitan*. Feedback from readers comes from articles that are about what people *think* about, and not profiles. Breasts get a lot of mail and feminine hygiene deodorants get a lot.

LASKY: How about the reaction from the *Esquire* piece you did on Helen Gurley Brown? What did Helen Gurley Brown do?

EPHRON: She was very unhappy. She was upset about two things basically. First, I said that *Cosmo* published the worst work of the good writers. And she was *very* upset about that. She wrote me a letter because she was so upset. I still think I am right so it's a point on which we still differ. She was also furious at the picture that *Esquire* printed with it, which really was not a nice picture. She wrote the editor a letter telling him that he was a shit for using that picture. He called me and asked if I thought it was a bad picture. And I told him it was right, but that he was at *Esquire* too long when he didn't know when he was being cruel to people. But then, a few days after all of that mail, I got a letter from Helen's *husband*, who said that sometimes the subjects of interviews are the last to know when a piece has caught them, and you really got her. That made me feel good. Then Helen wrote three days later saying, "Okay, I've calmed down and I still don't like that line but it's okay. I am not unhappy."

LASKY: Do you ever feel guilty after you've put someone down?

EPHRON: Sure. And sometimes I don't put people down. Some things I hold back. I know it's so easy to hurt someone. But as Lillian Hellman said to me in an interview I had with her recently, "All that anyone remembers is the slightest word of reservation you write about them." It's true.

FEMINIST WITH A FUNNY BONE

INTERVIEW BY PATRICK McGILLIGAN
BACKSTORY 5: INTERVIEWS WITH SCREENWRITERS OF THE 1990S
JUNE 2007

Nora Ephron has several careers, which she has shuffled like a master dealer always with one more card up her sleeve.

Long before her first screen credit, she was well known as one of the leading voices of New Journalism, a tough reporter, first-person essayist, and feminist with a funny bone—sometimes one or the other, other times all three at once. Three collections of her newspaper and magazine pieces became bestselling books in the 1970s. Her first marriage was to writer Dan Greenburg; her second was newsworthy: Carl Bernstein, one of the two Washington Post *reporters who pushed the Watergate story until Nixon resigned. (The disintegration of their marriage was channeled into Ephron's first novel,* Heartburn, *later filmed by Mike Nichols from a script by Ephron.) High on the who's who of East Coast literary lights, she even appeared as a party guest in two Woody Allen films.*

When she turned to scriptwriting in the early 1980s, Ephron was, in a sense, coming home to Hollywood. Her personal backstory included a childhood growing up in Los Angeles, as the oldest of four daughters of Henry and Phoebe Ephron, who together wrote plays like Take Her, She's Mine *and a number of sparkling motion pictures, including* There's No Business Like Show Business *(1954), the screen version of* Carousel *(1956), and the Hepburn–Tracy comedy* Desk Set *(1957), capping their scriptwriting careers with an Oscar nomination for adapting*

Captain Newman, M.D. *in 1964. We Thought We Could Do Anything: The Life of Screenwriters Phoebe and Henry Ephron (1977) is Henry Ephron's elegant memoir of the family's life out west, with a moving introduction by Nora and many glimpses of her precocity as a child. Her parents were displaced New Yorkers, and she did not much like California (or Hollywood). After an education at Wellesley, she ended up in New York working for newspapers, which she highly recommends for budding scenarists looking for better training than film school.*

After dipping her toes in television in the late 1970s, she was asked by director Mike Nichols to write a true-life script about the suspicious car-crash death of antinuclear crusader and union activist Karen Silkwood. The gritty, disturbing Silkwood, *which starred Meryl Streep (who later played the Ephron character in the film* Heartburn*), brought Ephron her first Oscar nomination in 1983.* Silkwood *performed only modestly at the box office compared to the hilarious romantic comedy* When Harry Met Sally . . . , *which was a runaway crowd pleaser in 1989, swiftly achieving iconic status among writers as well as fans, for its smart script probing the limits of platonic friendship between a man (Harry, played by Billy Crystal) and a woman (Sally, played by Meg Ryan) who are sexually attracted to each other. (Everyone knows the scene in the crowded Katz's Deli, where Harry is insisting he can't be fooled by a woman's pretend orgasm. Sally, loudly and vividly, fakes one to win the argument, topped by—it was Billy Crystal's suggestion, which Ephron added to the script—a woman customer shouting out, "I'll have what she's having!") Ephron collected a second Oscar nomination for this film.*

She crashed the boy's club of directing in 1992 with This Is My Life, *based on a Meg Wolitzer novel about a single mother finding a second chance in stand-up comedy. Then she was called in on an informal remake of Leo McCarey's* An Affair to Remember *(1957), and her witty final script (again, Oscar-nominated) and growingly assured direction transformed* Sleepless in Seattle *into the perfect date movie of 1993.*

During the 1980s, Alice Arlen was her regular collaborator; on more recent projects younger sister Delia has served in that capacity. Things came full circle in 1998 when Ephron reunited Sleepless in Seattle *stars Tom Hanks and Meg Ryan in* You've Got Mail, *the Ephron sisters' Internet-themed update of Ernst Lubitsch's* The Shop Around the Corner *(1940); one of their parents' earliest jobs in Hollywood had been on the last Lubitsch film (*That Lady in Ermine, *1948) before the master of sophisticated comedy died.*

*Along the way there has been a kooky-teenager-with-mobster-dad drama (*Cookie, *1989); the underrated* My Blue Heaven *(1990) and* Mixed Nuts *(1994), both starring Steve Martin;* Michael *(1996), which features John Travolta as an angel luring all the women out on the floor of a roadhouse for a magical dance to "Chain of Fools";* Hanging Up *(2000), an adaptation with Delia of her sister's novel for the actress—and in this instance, director—Diane Keaton; another Travolta vehicle,* Lucky Numbers *(2000), which is the only time Ephron has directed a film from someone else's script; and the big-screen version of TV's* Bewitched *(2005), with Nicole Kidman and Will Ferrell, which inexplicably fizzled.*

*Her comedies embrace the McCarey–Lubitsch tradition, albeit with a hip female sensibility. Her journalistic dramas have proven harder to sell to an increasingly homogenized Hollywood. Lately she's shifted her energies into a play (*Imaginary Friends,

about the relationship, anything but friendly, between novel-
ist-essayist Mary McCarthy and playwright Lillian Hellman),
and to fresh journalism (leading to another bestselling book, I
Feel Bad About My Neck: And Other Thoughts on Being
a Woman, *in 2006). She still prefers New York, where she lives*
with her husband, crime writer Nicholas Pileggi, who is also an
*occasional screenwriter (*Goodfellas*).*

In the spirit of You've Got Mail, *this interview was con-*
ducted by e-mail.

McGILLIGAN: You once said that a helpful strategy for you as
a journalist was to write as though you were writing a letter to
your mother and then lop off the salutation. I have a feeling
that strategy doesn't work as well for film, even though your
mother—and father—were scriptwriters. Who is your imagined ideal reader for any script that you are writing? (And is it
the same as your imagined audience for the film?)

EPHRON: Actually, I didn't exactly say that. (Although who
knows?) What I hope I said is that my mother used to quote
George Bernard Shaw, who may or may not have said, The
best way to learn to write is to write a letter to your mother and
cut off the "Dear Mom." Just quoting that makes me know
absolutely that George Bernard Shaw never said anything of
the kind. But my mother definitely did, and definitely at-
tributed it to someone. No question it was very helpful to me
in becoming a journalist, in that becoming comfortable with
your voice is part of what makes it possible to write a column,
make a joke in print, etc.

I don't think it works at all in screenwriting, though. But I suspect I've always had ideal readers for my scripts, though different ideal readers for each one. (The same was true when I became a columnist and magazine writer, I always had an ideal reader.)

No question that my ideal reader for screenplays was often Mike Nichols, because I learned so much about screenwriting from him. And occasionally (in the case of *You've Got Mail*) the ideal reader was Tom Hanks, because I hoped he would play the lead, and because I learned so much about screenwriting from him. When I wrote *When Harry Met Sally . . .* , I was writing it for Rob Reiner, whose idea it was—so he was my ideal reader.

McGILLIGAN: Although you are a "child of Hollywood," you spent years in journalism and a long time in doing other things before coming around to film. There aren't many "children of Hollywood" who are second- or third-generation screenwriters. It's as though, early on, you (and they) had become hyper-aware of the pitfalls. In your case, what took you so long? I have a suspicion it wasn't merely happenstance.

EPHRON: Well, I never wanted to be in the movie business when I was growing up. For one thing, it would have meant living in Los Angeles. No one in the movie business in the 1950s lived anywhere else. I would have died if I'd had to live in Los Angeles. From the moment we moved there for good, in 1946, when I was five, I knew a terrible mistake had been made. For another thing, I didn't want to be in the movie business, I wanted to be a journalist. It was only after I'd been a journalist for years that I tried screenwriting. By then, you could live in New York and be in the movie business, thank God.

McGILLIGAN: In what I like to refer to as the "so-called golden age" of Hollywood, many scriptwriters honed their writing skills on newspapers and magazines. Today Hollywood is flooded with film (and business) school graduates. Few screenwriters come from journalism. Journalism itself isn't what it used to be, but it's like Hollywood has dropped it as part of the curriculum. And I feel that not only are their fewer "journalistic" movies, but that the lack of scriptwriters with a newspaper background contributes to the homogenization of scripts and films. Do you agree? What is the most important thing you learned as a journalist, that helps with every script?

EPHRON: I always tell kids who want to go to film school that they should become journalists instead. And I always tell journalists they should write screenplays. But no one listens to me. What I loved about journalism is that you learn a great deal about all the things you write about; in my case I was very lucky, and wrote about pretty much everything: crimes, politics, fluff, famous people, New York, heat waves, real estate, the women's movement, journalism, to name a few. Then, if you want to write screenplays, you at least know something about something.

When Alice Arlen and I wrote *Silkwood*, I knew all sorts of things—how to report a story, most importantly. But I also knew about unions because I'd been active in the Newspaper Guild at the *New York Post*. And I knew what people talked about at work. And I also understood structure in an instinctive way, because one of the things you learn as a magazine journalist is Beginning, Middle, End, which is pretty much the main thing you have to understand when you write a screenplay.

McGILLIGAN: There are still numerous "films based on true-life events," but not many feel true to life and there are often sentimental script contrivances. Films like *Silkwood*, in which you honestly "report a story," are few and far between (if not virtually extinct in Hollywood) nowadays. What is the special responsibility of such a script, based on actual characters and events?

EPHRON: My feelings is that these scripts have a real responsibility to—well, not to facts, because there are very few real "facts"—but to certain things that you simply can't change because (as Richard Nixon once put it) it would be wrong.

You can't write *Silkwood* and make Karen Silkwood into a saint. She wasn't a saint. One of the things that was hard for me at the beginning with *Silkwood*, by the way, was that most of the journalism that had been written about her had been one-sided, either painting her as a saint or as a hysteric. When Alice Arlen and I interviewed Karen's boyfriend, Drew Stevens, he told us that she had flashed her breasts one day in the plutonium plant, and I suddenly understood her. Having Meryl Streep involved with the project from the beginning was also very helpful, because we knew that she would be able to play a complicated young woman and so we were going to be free to write one.

Anyway, my feeling is that when you write a story that's based on actual characters and events, there are certain marks you have to hit, that you have an obligation to, even as a screenwriter. So in the case of Karen Silkwood, you had to make her complicated, you had to make her difficult, and obviously, there were certain factual moments that you absolutely had to include. But there's no rule; you sort of know what they are. On the other hand, Alice and I seriously fiddled with the length of time involved. The movie takes events that took place over a couple of years and makes them into a much shorter time period. Alice is brilliant at structure, among other things, and this was very much her idea.

McGILLIGAN: You say that you preferred journalism, early on, and at first had no intentions of writing films. I know you did some interesting television, starting out, but what is it exactly (or as exactly as you might be able to say) that ultimately made you turn to scriptwriting?

EPHRON: I didn't do any interesting television. I did a script for a women's caper movie that sold to television. It was the first thing I did that was produced, and it wasn't good.

What mostly made me turn to screenwriting is that everyone in New York was sort of trying to get into screenwriting. Carl Bernstein and I had done some work on the script of *All the President's Men* (1976) in a misguided attempt to convey to Alan Pakula and Robert Redford some of the things that he and Bob Woodward felt were missing from the original draft. Someone saw the work I'd done and suggested I write a women's caper movie, which I did. And it wasn't a good movie but it wasn't a bad script, so I started to get work as a screenwriter. Which was lucky.

McGILLIGAN: Can you characterize what Mike Nichols taught you?

EPHRON: He taught me many, many things. Here are two: (1) To look at each scene of the movie and say, "What is this section of the movie called?" And whatever the answer is, that's what the scene had to be about. And if six scenes in a row are all called the same thing, then you'd better fix that because you have too many scenes that are all about the same thing. (2) To free-associate whenever you work on a scene. So if the scene is about a breakup, you should basically think about all the breakups you've known. The same goes for falling in love, or betrayal, or whatever. It's a way of using psychoanalysis and writing together, and it is, of course, the reason why Mike Nichols's breakup with one of his girlfriends ended up in *Silkwood.*

McGILLIGAN: Why, after *Silkwood* (and, to an extent, *Heartburn*), does it seem, at least judging from your official credits, that you left "reportorial" and "journalistic" films behind? Is that to some extent because of Hollywood and what the market will bear? Changing times, happenstance? Or did you write other hard-hitting, true-story scripts that weren't filmed?

EPHRON: I have written two scripts that are reportorial. One about Maggie Higgins, who won a Pulitzer Prize for covering the Korean War for the *New York Herald-Tribune*. Alice Arlen and I wrote it together, and it is one of the heartbreaks of my life as a screenwriter that it was never made. It came this close several times. The other is called "Stories About McAlary," about a man named Mike McAlary who also won a Pulitzer, writing for the *Daily News*. I hope that Home Box Office is going to make it.

McGILLIGAN: It also seems that with *When Harry Met Sally . . .* , you came "home" to a strong suit that had been waiting for you to take it up. To some extent, "home" to the tradition of your parents (with films like *Desk Set*) and the evergreen tradition of romantic comedy. Can you talk about how and why you got the job, and how the project started out, versus how it ended up?

EPHRON: The idea for it was Rob Reiner's: let's do a movie about two people who become friends at the end of the first major relationships of their lives, and make a decision not to have sex because it ruins the relationship, and then they have sex and it ruins the relationship. That's where it began. I interviewed Rob and Andy Scheinman (the producer) about their lives as single men, and basically approached the script as an essay on being single. Then, around the third draft or so, they interviewed me, and that's where the orgasm scene began. There is quite a long description of the whole thing in the introduction to the published screenplay of *When Harry Met Sally . . .*

The orgasm scene was, of course, started by Rob and Andy and me, made into legend by Meg Ryan (whose idea it was for Sally to have the orgasm at the end of the scene), and by Billy Crystal (who thought of the line "I'll have what she's having"). I learned in the course of that movie that if an actor wants to change something for the better, you would have to be a fool to object.

McGILLIGAN: Are you conscious, having at one time described yourself as a radical feminist (I'm sure you're the same now, only different), of always struggling with the clichés of romantic comedy? After all, you once wrote, "So many of the conscious and unconscious ways men and women treat each other have to do with romantic and sexual fantasies that are deeply ingrained, not just in society but in literature." And of course Hollywood plays a big part!

EPHRON: When did I describe myself as a radical feminist? I'm a feminist but never a radical feminist, to the best of my memory. But yet I still agree with that quote. And of course Hollywood plays a big part. That's one of the subjects in all my romantic comedies—the role of other movies (or, in the case of *You've Got Mail*, books) in that fantasy.

McGILLIGAN: It's interesting when you talk about the contribution of Billy Crystal to *When Harry Met Sally* . . . I can't help but notice you are fond of casting other actors who were once stand-up comedians and who might be counted on to be freewheeling with their ideas and performances: Steve Martin, Dan Aykroyd, Tom Hanks, even Will Ferrell. Do your comedy scripts in particular remain fluid for the actors?

EPHRON: Tom Hanks was never a stand-up comedian, and Rob Reiner cast Billy Crystal in *When Harry Met Sally . . .* But many actors who are funny began as stand-up comedians, so you inevitably (when casting someone funny) are going to cast people who began as stand-up comedians. I learned on *When Harry Met Sally . . .* that you have to remain open to change, especially when you're directing comedy. What's the point of casting all these people who are comedically gifted if you don't take advantage of their brilliance at comedy and improvisation?

When I started out as a screenwriter, everyone knew about the legendary screenwriter Paddy Chayefsky, whose contract stipulated that you could not change one word of his screenplay. Everyone thought this was a goal worth having, contract-wise. But after I worked with Rob and Billy and Meg on *When Harry Met Sally . . .* , it crossed my mind that Chayevsky had no understanding at all of the movie-making process.

McGILLIGAN: Every time I quote something you said in the past I seem to get it a little wrong, but in one of your long-ago profiles, you wrote about a pioneering lady umpire (I think) and the "ridicule and abuse" women must undergo when they pioneer in a male-dominated profession. I can't think of a more male-dominated profession than directing motion pictures, still. Why did you take up that job?

EPHRON: Well, being the first woman umpire is very different from being a director, and I was hardly the first woman director. The hardest thing about being a woman director is not the directing part—and if you have a crew that's good and you are careful not to hire Australian cameramen and you're prepared, you'll be fine. But the hard part is getting movies made that are not slamdunk action pictures, which most women don't direct and (in my case) aren't interested in directing.

McGILLIGAN: You said you "learned" a lot about screenwriting from Tom Hanks during *Sleepless in Seattle*. Can you tell me more about that? And at what stage did you take over the script and directing?

EPHRON: I came onto *Sleepless* to do a three-week polish for a director who was already attached to a go-picture with actors who were semi-cast. At least three writers had been on the project before me. The script I polished was not a comedy, it was sort of gloopy, but it had all sorts of things about it that worked, particularly the ending at the Empire State Building. I made it funny and basically made the woman's part better and the kid's part better. When I turned it in, there was sort of a feeding frenzy for the script—a huge number of actors wanted to be in it. Everyone loved it. I've never had anything quite like it happen. Everyone loved it except for the director who was attached, so he withdrew.

So the people at Tri-Star asked me if I wanted to direct it, and long story short, I said yes. As for the actors—the actress also withdrew, perhaps understanding that she was not funny, which she isn't; and the actor, who hadn't made a deal to be in the movie, was just shunted aside in favor of Tom. But Tom felt that his part was underwritten—which it was, by the way, and he didn't commit until he and I and Delia had spent quite a lot of time together going scene by scene through the script. All sorts of great things in the script of *Sleepless* came from Tom's mouth in those meetings, including much of the best part of his phone call with Dr. Marsha, the radio talk-show host. But what I learned from Tom was a thing that's really important, which is that scene after scene, you have to give the main actor something to play, he can never be passive in the scene, et cetera, even (or especially) when he's sharing it with a very cute little boy.

McGILLIGAN: Can you talk a little about collaborating on scripts with your sister Delia? The fun or unique chemistry of it? I can't think of too many other female-sibling partnerships nowadays. It's almost like channeling your parents!

EPHRON: I love working with Delia because she makes me laugh more than anyone I know. I started working with her on the first movie I directed—*This Is My Life.* I had by then deluded myself into thinking that I had been wildly helpful to the directors I'd worked with as a screenwriter, and in any case, I wanted to make sure someone was there playing that role for me when I started directing. I knew for sure, in addition, that I'd need someone to make changes and have a cold clear eye out for the script. When you start directing, you really aren't looking out for the script—you're elsewhere. Anyway, it turned out to be exactly what I'd hoped for, and a chance for me to spend way more time than I normally would with one of my favorite people.

"I REMEMBER NOTHING": NORA EPHRON ON LIFE, DEATH, AND HOT DOGS

INTERVIEW BY KERRY LAUERMAN
SALON
NOVEMBER 7, 2010

The night before my planned interview with Nora Ephron, I sat before the TV watching our probable new speaker of the House, John Boehner, fawn and burble over his newfound success. Something gnawed, a prickly déjà vu. It wasn't until the next day, on my way back to the office after talking with Ephron, that I realized I had been thinking about a famous line from Ephron's Heartburn, *which popped up immediately when I went searching for it: "Beware of men who cry. It's true that men who cry are sensitive to and in touch with their feelings, but the only feelings they tend to be sensitive to and in touch with are their own."*

*Ephron is like that. After nearly fifty years as an author, screenwriter (*When Harry Met Sally . . . , Silkwood*), director (*Julie & Julia, Sleepless in Seattle*), her cultural influence is so elemental you're not always even aware of it; she's like hydrogen. But what makes her new book of essays,* I Remember Nothing—*along with its predecessor, the bestselling 2008 collection,* I Feel Bad About My Neck—*such a particularly big deal is not just that Ephron (who, full disclosure, I know a little socially) is a defining cultural voice, it's that she's now frequently tackling subjects—the infuriating inevitability of getting old, and facing death—without the gauzy sentimentality or spiritual superiority we're used to from others.*

In her new collection, Ephron writes movingly about her love of journalism, and takes us through a riveting account of her rise from a wildly misogynistic Newsweek *and through a rollicking New Journalism. Ephron remains a journalistic pioneer, and will be leading* The Huffington Post'*s forthcoming section devoted to a subject—divorce—that she's been inextricably linked to since* Heartburn, *her roman à clef about her failed marriage to Watergate great Carl Bernstein. There's an essay on divorce in* I Remember Nothing, *as well as short takes that touch on another favorite Ephron subject, food (chicken soup, egg whites, those infernal French dessert spoons). But the power of these essays often comes from a voice clearly looking back at a riveting life with a clear-eyed wisdom and, at times, twinges of regret.*

Salon *spoke with Ephron at her New York apartment last week.*

LAUERMAN: We're trained to talk about getting old and facing death by also talking about faith, but you're an atheist.

EPHRON: I said in the book that it would be helpful to believe in God. It would be helpful, but I certainly know I'm not going to be one of those people with a deathbed conversion.

LAUERMAN: Have you felt any of that tug as you've gotten older?

EPHRON: To faith?

LAUERMAN: Yes.

EPHRON: No. No, no, no. No, that would be ludicrous.

LAUERMAN: It's common, though. You must have known people who've been lifelong atheists or agnostics . . .

EPHRON: It's entirely possible that I know people that that's happened to, but they don't spring to my head.

I was thinking about this last night as I watched the elections returns come in, the endless babble about how angry people were, and I have such a sense of how insulated we are in New York City from whatever is going on out there. We really don't have a clue. And every so often I'm with a group of people and you just run out of things to say and I say, "How many people believe in God?" In fact, the way we play the game is you have to guess how many people at the table believe in God. And it's always more than I think it's going to be. I'm always a little surprised that it's even three out of eight.

LAUERMAN: Do a lot of people hedge?

EPHRON: Yes, they do. "I believe there's something." They do that. But the short answer to your question is no.

LAUERMAN: Well, one of the really powerful chapters of your book is a simple listing of things you'll miss when you're dead. It's incredible to read, because I don't think many people really go there; it's uncomfortable. But obviously, you have to have some awareness after you die to actually miss something.

EPHRON: Well, of course. But there's nothing wrong with knowing what you're going to miss beforehand so you have quite a lot of it before it's over. I mean this is one of the worst things I remember clearly when my friend Judy—whom I keep writing about because it was so devastating—was dying. She had tongue cancer. And she said one day, I'm not even going to be able to have my last meal. So it seems to me, Have your last meal all the time, because you have to know that the odds are very, very small that you'll be in the mood for a Nate 'n' Al's hot dog, which is my last meal.

LAUERMAN: That's in L.A.

EPHRON: Yes, and they FedEx.

LAUERMAN: You get them FedEx'd to you?

EPHRON: Oh, yeah.

LAUERMAN: Why are they so great?

EPHRON: You know, I feel really bad that you've never had one. First of all, they have a really lovely skin on them. Not too thick, but just right.

And they're garlicky, but not too garlicky. They're spicy, a little teeny bit, but not too spicy. They're the perfect size. I mean, everything about them is sort of platonically fabulous, as hot dogs go.

LAUERMAN: I'm glad you brought up your friend's death, because there are two really memorable essays about her in this book and your last one. There are different deaths in our lives that have much greater impact for whatever reason, either they're really young and it's their first face of mortality . . .

EPHRON: Yes, my grandfather.

LAUERMAN: Is that still very vivid to you?

EPHRON: No, I just had no idea what death was when my grandfather died. And I remember being told that grandpa was dead and thinking, Oh, that's sad. And then about a month later I was sick and I thought Grandpa was going to come over and play casino with me. And then I realized he wasn't, ever. And that was kind of that first child's idea of, Oh, that's what it means. He's not going to be there.

LAUERMAN: Was it accompanied by fear or just sadness?

EPHRON: No, just sadness. No, the thing with friends when you get older—I mean this is not anything I haven't written about—is they can't be replaced. When you're thirty, you accumulate friends and you shed friends and you get closer at certain moments to some than others. And you have a huge bench of friends. And then that's just not true.

LAUERMAN: So the reason you've written about your friend's death . . .

EPHRON: It's just that she was my very best friend. And that's that. There's never going to be another one. The person you can really talk to about anything. The person who knows your kids, whom your kids love, think of as family, all the things that happen over the years and that's gone. It's an amazing loss and almost everybody my age has that, that hole, where there used to be somebody.

LAUERMAN: You're at the age, too—and you write about this—when almost every week brings bad news. Do you become immune to it? Does it toughen you?

EPHRON: No, when it's someone you're really close to, not at all. No. But did you read the piece that Michael Kinsley did about illness and aging in *The New Yorker*? About how it's sort of the last piece of luck—or bad luck. I'm paraphrasing, but I just remember reading it and thinking, Oh, yes, that is so true.

LAUERMAN: Luck in what kind of way?

EPHRON: Some people just get unbelievably lucky and they're like Kitty Hart and they live to be ninety-four years old and still performing at Carnegie Hall. And still with great legs. And then . . .

LAUERMAN: But you've had good luck. The idea that you're seventy is shocking.

EPHRON: Thank you so much, thank you.

LAUERMAN: But does that help? You've been hearing that

since the last book, too, people can't believe you're worried about age.

EPHRON: Well, I know, but you'll see someday that of course you think that, because you're young. We have very little imagination about almost anything. That's the truth.

I remember being young and looking at a table of older women having lunch. This was back in the day when older women had gray hair. And they were having this fantastically animated lunch. And I remember thinking something like, Oh, look how much fun they're having. And they're so old! Now I realize they were probably younger than I am and, you know, it's one of the things that young people don't understand, that old people feel as if they're still young except in certain ways, which are all too horrible. Like the fact that you simply physically aren't what you used to be. But you really are the same person as you always were. And much wiser and yet not. But younger people have no sense at all about older people. None. No imagination at all.

LAUERMAN: You mention *Heartburn* in this book a few times, and note that it was forged out of a grief and painful—

EPHRON: No, no. Not a painful book to write. Going through [the divorce] was horrible. Writing about it wasn't horrible.

LAUERMAN: It was a product of going through this pain.

EPHRON: Yes. I knew, I knew I had a novel. I knew I had a something. If I could just find the voice to write and then one day I did. One day I just wrote the first eight or ten pages of it, just like that. But I couldn't have done that while it was happening.

LAUERMAN: Do you think you're at your funniest when you're writing about something that's been painful?

EPHRON: Not necessarily, but I do think that if you can convert a certain kind of . . . I'm already nervous about using the word "anger," because I'm not a particularly angry person, but I do think that underneath pieces like "I Feel Bad About My Neck" is some kind of actual anger about the aging process. Which then turns into a bunch of jokes. But I don't think all humor comes out of unhappiness or pain. There are simply too many funny people who had a completely, you know, normal childhood. Not necessarily happy, but who had a really happy childhood. Almost nobody worth knowing has a happy childhood.

LAUERMAN: I think there's always a portrait of you as very unflappable and impermeable. This is a very warm book. I'm wondering if that's something you've read about yourself from other people and you've taken notice of it.

EPHRON: Well, I think you know this: That very few people end up knowing who you are. I don't mean me. I just mean that most people are misunderstood in some way. I don't mean in a bad way. I just mean that they're not comprehended. But I don't really think about it a whole lot. And if I do think about it, I think I must do something to make them misunderstand me. But, what's for dinner?

LAUERMAN: Right. What can you do? You write about your start in journalism, at *Newsweek*, in a "Mad Men" era when there was this incredible male hierarchy, and you were stuck in—

EPHRON: —the girls' department.

LAUERMAN: The girls' department. I think it's an immensely confusing time for people who weren't there, because at the same time, you did have women like Lillian Ross, whom you write about in another essay, who was a big star at *The New Yorker*.

EPHRON: Well, there were exceptions to the rule. And I think there were always exceptions to the rule, fewer and fewer as you go back in time. But it was so clear in my house that we were all going to end up being writers. And that my extremely powerful, albeit eventually fairly wacky, parents would be disappointed in us if we weren't. And since our mother was a writer, you know, it all seemed like maybe this could be done, to me.

A friend of mine was a woman writer at *Time*—Josie Davis, who died very young—and you knew, therefore, that there weren't going to be any other [women] writers at *Time*. There was going to be one at a place. And the result of that was that there was a tremendous amount of submerged competition among the handful of us that were climbing the greasy pole. Because you really did think, Is she going to get it? Or am I? There was never any sense that there was room for all of you. It seems to me that a great deal of that is gone now.

LAUERMAN: You then entered probably the hottest era in American magazines, writing for both Harold Hayes's *Esquire* and Clay Felker's *New York*. Were there more women there?

EPHRON: Clay had lots of women. *Esquire* didn't have many and, by the way, still doesn't.

But when I watch *Mad Men*, it frustrates me so much, because it's 1964 and Don Draper is still wearing a hat? I don't think so! This is the stuff I get completely obsessed with.

LAUERMAN: In the book you talk about this, how it's a curse being older and knowing when the period details are wrong. Do they mistakenly have takeout pizza on *Mad Men*?

EPHRON: No, they don't. That was in *A Beautiful Mind*. In 1948, takeout pizza in Princeton, New Jersey. I don't think so.

LAUERMAN: Does that just stop you cold?

EPHRON: It does. And then if you say that to anyone connected with the movies, they say, If you're thinking that you're not really in the movie. And I go, Yeah, exactly. Exactly! That's what I'm trying to say to you.

LAUERMAN: I can't imagine you feel huge pangs of nostalgia seeing *Newsweek* teeter on the brink, but what do you think about the death, or pending demise, of some of these great publications?

EPHRON: I don't think I ever thought *Newsweek* was so important. *Esquire* is still with us. *New York* magazine is booming. *New York* is as good as it has ever been. I think I feel worse about places where I never worked.

LAUERMAN: But if you were graduating from college right now, where would you want to work?

EPHRON: I think I'd probably want to write for *New York* magazine.

LAUERMAN: Still.

EPHRON: Yeah, because print is still print. I found it fascinating that Tina Brown wanted to run a magazine, when she's done this great website. And we all know that Web is the future and print is the past, but you know, yeah sure. Even *Rolling Stone* I would be happy to write for. Even though I don't know anything about music.

LAUERMAN: But now you're a Web pioneer. Is it different? Is it exciting in different ways, writing for the Web?

EPHRON: Well, I just think for a handful of websites, you can't confuse what's on the Web with journalism. You know, [*Salon* has] actual journalism and there are a few other places that do. But mostly everybody else is just feeding off the carcass of *The New York Times*. So if I came to New York and wanted to be a journalist, I would want to work at a place where there's still journalism.

LAUERMAN: Were there any essays that were particularly tough to write?

EPHRON: Yes, yes, several of them. I would write them for a while, then just leave them unfinished.

LAUERMAN: The one about a famous story about a run-in between your mother and Lillian Ross that you were never quite sure was true or not.

EPHRON: The one about my mother and Lillian Ross was not so hard to write.

LAUERMAN: Really? I don't want to ruin it for anybody who will read it, but I thought it really tapped into a deep desire to justify hero worship in our parents. What made it easy to write, and why did you write about it now?

EPHRON: I think I was ready to write it. And believe me, if it were a triggering mechanism, I would not be able to tell you what it was, because I would have forgotten. But I don't remember having any struggle with it.

LAUERMAN: It's also just a great story.

EPHRON: Well, and it's always been a good story. And when it happened, when that part of it happened, when the pure Lillian Ross of it happened, it was such a coin dropping. It was such an amazing "Oh my god, this is an extraordinary thing." But I've obviously known it for thirty years and never quite written that thing about my mother. Because it's really about my mother.

LAUERMAN: Although you've written a lot about your mother.

EPHRON: I have indeed, yes.

LAUERMAN: Is that one of your favorite stories about her?

EPHRON: Oh, I don't know. I think we all have a lot of stories about her. I was the luckiest of the sisters because I was the eldest. My mother used to always say, "You are not the eldest, you are the oldest." But I had more good years than any of them.

LAUERMAN: Because her condition deteriorated after you left.

EPHRON: She just didn't really become an alcoholic until I was fourteen or fifteen years old.

LAUERMAN: You include a painful scene about when she came to visit you at Wellesley when you graduated, and how you just hoped that she wouldn't embarrass you.

EPHRON: Yes, but my sister Delia's stories about her are so much darker and more horrible than mine. She got left with it. I went off to college and Delia was left with it.

LAUERMAN: The other Lillian essay in the book is about your one-time friendship with Lillian Hellman, and your regret over how it ended.

EPHRON: That was a very weird thing, because in the course of writing, it all came back to me how much fun she was. That memory had been so buried in all the stuff she had done later and in the end of it, you know the relationship kind of ended in its own way.

LAUERMAN: You recount all the excuses you had for shunning her, and really they're all . . .

EPHRON: Perfectly good excuses.

LAUERMAN: Really good excuses.

EPHRON: I know, I know.

LAUERMAN: So is the sadness now at the way it ended a recent realization?

EPHRON: I had no idea I was going to end up there when I wrote it. I had no idea what it was. Sometimes you just say, I think I'll try writing about this and it doesn't work. There's a whole bunch of stuff that didn't work for this [book]. But that, I really didn't know where it was going. And it sat there for quite a while. Then I started rereading her letters that were in a drawer, and I just felt everything. I felt the "Oh this is so charming, oh this is so wonderful, oh I'm so lucky to get this, oh I'm so bored." There it all was. She was so divinely problematical until she was problematical. And I just hadn't come anywhere near all of that. And of course I wrote a play about her. So I had truly managed to push away any feelings I had toward her that might have made me feel guilty about having a certain amount of fun with her.

LAUERMAN: In a different essay, you talk about how getting old involves constantly thinking about reflecting on the great things, but also the little mistakes along the way that haunt you.

EPHRON: Or the big mistakes.

LAUERMAN: Or the big mistakes. Is that one of those little mistakes?

EPHRON: Well, I think I just feel that I could have been kinder. Big deal. You know? Especially when you're young, you're so puffed up with your standards. That's probably one of the only good things about being older is you have fewer and fewer standards.

LAUERMAN: Sure, and big deal, but at the same time, reading that essay in particular, it does make you think, Gosh, will there be a lot of that? Will there be a lot of looking back and going . . . oh.

EPHRON: Yes, there is. There is. That I can tell you.

LAUERMAN: Do you think it makes you a nicer person now?

EPHRON: No. Well, maybe it does. Maybe it does. You know. Somebody died this year, Daniel Schorr, whom I wrote about when he got fired by CBS [for *Esquire* in 1976]. And in retrospect, it's one of several things I've written in my life that I just think, Oh, get over yourself. Just really. How self-important could anyone have been. And he died and it just came marching back at me. Because you certainly write things when you are young, especially, that you just go, "Moving on . . ." It hurt someone's feelings and you just don't even think about it.

LAUERMAN: Last question. I imagine you love Thanksgiving. What's your go-to Thanksgiving dish?

EPHRON: You know, we've now aced the turkey.

LAUERMAN: Do you really like turkey?

EPHRON: I love turkey. I love it. In fact, I'm having turkey pangs right now, because it's time for turkey. But you don't ever have turkey from October 1 to November something, because . . .

LAUERMAN: It might ruin it.

EPHRON: It might ruin it. But we've discovered the way to cook a turkey, which I'm going to bore you with. Which is you take the turkey and you salt and pepper it, and you can put Lowry's seasoning salt on it if you want to, and you stick it in the pan at 450 and you do not do one thing to it. You don't baste it, you don't . . .

LAUERMAN: Do you cover it?

EPHRON: You might have to cover it at a certain point. And you might have to drain some of the fat that comes off, but it's all these years of endless basting for nothing, it turns out.

LAUERMAN: So your revelation is to do nothing.

EPHRON: Yes.

THE LAST INTERVIEW

INTERVIEW BY KATHRYN BOREL
THE BELIEVER
MARCH 2012

Nora Ephron says that when she's writing a movie, the middle is the hardest part to get right. But in real life, and socially, she's great at the middle. She'll even substitute it for the beginning, which has the captivating effect of fostering an immediate sense of social intimacy.

We met on a day when the leaves were starting to crumble off L.A.'s deciduous trees and blow all over the place. As she pulled open the heavy wooden door to her bright, neat home in Beverly Hills, before extending her hand or saying hello, she looked past me at the ground and said something about how she was happy there were no leaves on the front steps, that she didn't want it to be messy for my arrival. A little later, after giving me coffee and water to drink, and corn chips to eat, she motioned to a small bowl of satsuma tangerines on the table. She was already eating one and said, "You have to try one. They're from my little tree." Before I could pick one out of the bowl, she peeled off two segments from hers and placed them in my palm.

There's a practicality to her charisma that is rare, though that shouldn't come as a surprise to anyone who has followed her enormous career. Ephron has been working in male-dominated milieus since her early twenties: starting with newspaper journalism in New York in the 1960s; moving on to magazine writing, then screenplays; accruing a hat trick of Academy Award nominations for writing Silkwood, When Harry Met Sally . . . , *and* Sleepless in Seattle, *which she also directed. Her latest success was* Julie & Julia, *which she wrote, produced, and directed.*

Her 2006 book, I Feel Bad About My Neck: And Other Thoughts on Being a Woman, *became a bestseller, as did her follow-up essay collection,* I Remember Nothing: And Other Reflections. *Critics and fans recognize her as the mother of the romantic comedy, and a whole other subset of critics and fans credits her with being the original Tina Fey. But she's likely to reject all that lionizing—of her career, her accolades, her voice. It became clear over the course of our conversation that every bit of her work energy goes not into mythology, nor the crusade of the female comedy writer, but into the slog of writing, thinking, planning, and more writing.*

I
GRAMMATICALLY INCORRECT
MORAL OUTRAGE

BOREL: You've said that as you get further into your career, you become afraid of repeating yourself, of repeating narratives. What exercises do you undertake to keep your brain churning out fresh material?

EPHRON: One exercise is to write. That's one of the reasons I became interested in blogging—it was a new muscle to flex. I mean, I'm not even sure it is any longer, because things move very quickly in internet culture, but six years ago it was a new form. It wasn't quite an essay, but it was essayish. It had to be short because of the concentration span of the reader. It had a different function from other kinds of writing, in that it wasn't meant to just be this piece of writing that people read, it was meant to be a piece of writing that started a conversation among the readers. Which became a reason for people to read it, so that they could then express what they thought about it. And once you learn that about blogging, then you first of all have the sense not to read any of the comments— because at a certain point they will be mean about you.

BOREL: Right. And they'll always invoke Hitler at some point, according to Godwin's law of Nazi Analogies.

EPHRON: Yeah! Or totally miss the joke. That's a given.

BOREL: The internet is the superhighway of grammatically incorrect moral outrage.

EPHRON: The thing is, you don't really have to believe what you write in a blog for more than the moment when you're writing it. You don't bring the same solemnity that you would bring to an actual essay. You don't think, Is this what I *really* want to say? You think, This is what I feel like saying at *this* moment. So that's one way to stay fresh. But there's no question in my mind . . . I sometimes feel like I don't have a thought that I haven't already written at some point in my life. [*Pause*] I don't mean that exactly. I honestly do have an original idea now and then. But there is a kind of sense of: If I were writing a column once a week, oh my god, I'd shoot myself! But the people who *do* do it are my writing heroes. I just can't get over how hard that is. People like Maureen Dowd and Gail Collins . . . My jaw is on the floor thinking of what it would be like to have to think of that many ideas. When I was at *Esquire* I did a monthly column, and that was about as many ideas as I had a year. About twelve ideas. There's no question that writing for a monthly is different than writing for a weekly. That's just the truth.

You know, the older I get, the more I understand what [Marshall] McLuhan meant when he said, "The medium is the message." I didn't really get it at all when I first read it, and now I'm very conscious of it. For instance, when I read a book on a Kindle, I've noticed that I'm more impatient. Because I'm turning the page so often, if something hasn't happened, I think, When is anything going to *happen* in this book? You become way more obsessed with plot than you would if you had an actual book and you understood where you were in that book. That little percentage tracker on the bottom of the Kindle screen is not a helpful thing. You can't go back when you've forgotten who a character is. So I'm very conscious of how that medium changes the reading experience completely.

II
FINDING VOICES

BOREL: What do you think of Arthur Quiller-Couch's "seven basic plots" theory? Or André Bazin's quote about how a great painter makes the same painting his entire life? Or that Woody Allen has made the same movie umpteen times?

EPHRON: I think if you're lucky enough to find a voice in whatever you do, that voice will come sneaking out no matter what. So I certainly think that's true. But I don't think for one second that Woody Allen has made the same movie over and over again.

BOREL: Having spent the last while reading most of your essays and watching your movies, I came to the conclusion that your two greatest skills are that you elevate the minute to make it interesting, and you ground the tragic to make it relatable. I feel like those are the hallmarks of your voice.

EPHRON: [*Laughs*] Thank you. I'm happy to hear this.

BOREL: Do you think you were born with that voice?

EPHRON: No. I think, for instance, that Joan Didion found her voice very early. She may have been born with her voice. When she was very young and writing at *Vogue*, you could look at a paragraph and say, "No one else could have written this but her." I don't think I came anywhere near that. And, by the way, I don't think anyone ever looks at my stuff and says, "No one could've written that but her!" I did not feel comfortable with a "voice" until I had been a journalist for seven or eight years.

BOREL: Was there a particular piece that caused you to think, This is it; I've really hit on something?

EPHRON: When I was at the *New York Post,* I covered the things you cover at the *New York Post*: trials and murders and the wedding of Luci Baines Johnson. I did everything. And then at a certain point they wanted to offer me a column. That was a huge deal; I was about twenty-four. And I spent about three weeks trying to write something, and I couldn't do it. It was a total failure! I just said to them, "I don't know how to do this. I'm not good at this."

BOREL: Why not?

EPHRON: I don't think I was "me" yet. I think I was still floundering around in all sorts of ways. I really did not know how to do it. I was at the *Post* for five years, then I was a freelance writer, and then when *Esquire* offered me a column, when I was thirtyish, I was ready. I've always felt that one of the mistakes people make is that they try to do something that is just slightly beyond their skill set, and then feel they've failed. When the *Post* hired me, I was twenty-two. They knew I had never been a newspaper reporter. They started me slow, with three-hundred-word pieces. Then I did slightly longer pieces, and I'd been there a year before I got to do what they called a "page piece," which was about twelve hundred words.

BOREL: Slowly for you, maybe, but you were still in New York City. It's not as though you started in Muncie, Indiana.

EPHRON: Well, I knew enough not to go get a job as a reporter at some little newspaper outside of New York and hope that someone would knock on my door one day . . .

BOREL: And present you with a job at *The New York Times,* tied up in a bow.

EPHRON: I just inched my way forward, and by the time I left the *Post* I was absolutely shot. I couldn't write one more piece of that sort. So when I started writing movies, which was in '75 or '76, I was ready to do that. It was fun to go into something I really knew nothing about.

BOREL: And to be writing fiction all of a sudden . . .

EPHRON: Yes, absolutely! The only way to learn is to keep doing something new, and, if you're lucky, learning with people who really know how to do it. People who will say, "No, no, no! Let's turn this scene over," or "Let's try this, let's do that, let's talk about breakups so we can make this breakup better." You know, all this stuff I learned from Mike Nichols.

BOREL: Screenwriting is very specific in terms of its structure. Journalistic work is slightly looser. Did you have any difficulties adapting to that more rigid format?

EPHRON: The fundamental thing that's true of both is that there's a beginning, a middle, and an end. What I really understood as a magazine writer was when the beginning had to start to end, and the middle had to begin, and when the middle had to start to end, and when the ending had to begin. And if you know that, you're halfway to being a screenwriter. People who go to those seminars with—

BOREL: Robert McKee—

EPHRON: And they know there are, let's say, seventy-six "master scenes" . . . I don't even know if a "master scene" is an expression! But it's all broken down mathematically, and I don't understand any of that.

BOREL: Really?

EPHRON: I don't do it. I never have done it. All that stuff that you learn about act structure, and scene structure, that every scene has three acts, all that stuff . . . I knew very instinctively from magazine writing.

BOREL: And by the time you had left the *Post* and were writing for magazines, you were no longer "floundering," as you said earlier. You had found your voice.

EPHRON: Sure—and all that material that ended up in *Wallflower at the Orgy*. But the great thing about the *Post* was that—unlike *The New York Times*—in that period you were allowed to be whatever you were. You weren't allowed to be right-wing, that was certainly true, but you were allowed to be a sort of left-wing nut or a sort of funny person. I remember covering those Johnson-girl weddings with at least 150 other people, most of them women, and they were basically writing about how many raisins were in the fruitcake. I was the only one who would write it as this hilarious cultural event instead of taking it completely seriously. I had an editor there named Stan Opotowsky, and he was always coming up with these great ideas for me. He would say, "Go out and find the most expensive apartment for rent in New York and report on it!" And I thought, Oh, I'm going to do this forever! I'm never going to want to do anything but this! [*Laughs*]

III
HAPPY ENDINGS, UNHAPPY MIDDLES

BOREL: Have you ever had a project that felt impossible to finish?

EPHRON: Yes. Oh, definitely. Several screenplays. God, yes.

BOREL: Is there a part of the screenplay that you find the most difficult?

EPHRON: The middle!

BOREL: Because that's when all the stuff has to happen?

EPHRON: The middle is the hard part, yes. The beginning and the end are the easy parts.

BOREL: I was expecting you to say endings, for some reason. I feel like it's tricky to draw out an ending, to resist the temptation not to cram all the solutions into the last ten minutes.

EPHRON: I can never make my endings very long. When we were doing *When Harry Met Sally . . .* the ending was about seven pages.

BOREL: Are you an advocate of happy endings?

EPHRON: I don't mean to get boring here, but I have written things that don't have happy endings. My closet is full of sad little scripts that didn't get made that have sad endings. It's very hard to get a movie made these days that has a sad ending. Or to get a sad movie made. [*Laughs*] It's very hard to get a movie made.

BOREL: Were you ever robbed of your ability to write because of overwhelmingly sad moments?

EPHRON: No. I've had friends who occasionally call and say, "I'm blocked!" And I've said, "Well, how are you going to pay the rent?" To me it was so obvious, you just had to work through it. In the old days, I would just type the piece over and over in the hopes that it would somehow push me into the next sentence. But you don't do that anymore with computers.

BOREL: Do you have little exercises you do these days when it's not coming as easily as you want it to?

EPHRON: I think one thing that you do is just make notes. You have to sit in a period called "not-writing" and write pages and pages of anything that crosses your mind. Or you can read things that will help you. I just did a script that has *Pride and Prejudice* as one of its themes . . .

BOREL: *Lost in Austen.*

EPHRON: Right. And I read the book a zillion times, and I did a kind of outline of the book, and in the end I used absolutely none of it except maybe the first six chapters. But the point is you do *something,* whether or not it's the actual writing. When I work with my sister Delia, we outline everything we're doing. Completely. The outlines are endless, at least fifty pages long. But when I write by myself, I almost never have an outline; I just do it. I know the structure. I know the beginning, the middle, the end.

BOREL: Do you do that with Delia so that there are no arguments during the process?

EPHRON: Yes.

BOREL: When did you learn that you have to do that when you're writing with her?

EPHRON: I did it with Alice Arlen first, on *Silkwood.* Collaboration is a tricky thing. There's always a negotiating point in collaboration. But when you're basing it on something else, on real-life events, there are givens. Karen Silkwood worked here, died here, had a boyfriend who she broke up with, had a roommate . . . All that stuff was a given, so Alice and I couldn't argue about it. But I could never have written *When Harry Met Sally* . . . with anyone else.

BOREL: Because it was all already in your head?

EPHRON: Yeah. I mean, it wasn't based on anything.

BOREL: Do you ever apply a screenplay structure to your own life? Has a part of your life reminded you of act three?

EPHRON: No. But I definitely divide my life into decades. Almost every ten years, something in my work life has changed. My twenties were my journalistic phase, then there was my screenwriting phase, then I became a director, then I started doing some plays . . .

BOREL: You have a strange number of pioneering, ambitious women in your family. Your sisters are successful writers, your mother was one of the few working female screenwriters in Hollywood at the time, and your mother's aunt was the first female dentist ever?

EPHRON: Allegedly!

BOREL: Do you think your ambition was innate or imparted?

EPHRON: I don't know. Part of it was that in my house, unlike 99.9 percent of all women our age, we were basically instructed to go out and have careers. Especially if you have a mother who's as powerful as ours was—and as simultaneously withholding—or powerful on account of that, who knows which . . . But part of your ambition comes from a desire to please her. Long after she is on the planet, by the way. So that's part of it. But there's no question I really wanted to be a newspaper reporter. And I really wanted to get a movie made. And I really wanted to direct a movie. If you don't want something, it's hard—in the movie business, especially. Sometimes I speak at film schools, and I speak to rooms of women. And they're very, very nice women, but you can see that they don't understand that it takes this huge amount of will and energy for anything to happen to you.

BOREL: Have you noticed an evolution of how your ambition has been received? In the 1970s versus the '80s or '90s? I wonder if it was more punishing to be an ambitious woman in the 1970s, even though there are still myriad ways in which ambitious women are punished.

EPHRON: Do you think it's ambitious women or successful women? I think you're very safe as an ambitious woman if you haven't succeeded.

BOREL: Then let's change the term to "successful women."

EPHRON: I think there's no question that women are jealous of other women, and men of course have their own problems with women. It's a weird thing because it's a fact, and yet you have to behave as if it's not a fact. Here's the given: It's really hard for women. People are going to attack you in a way that feels more virulent than it does with men. And you have to know what you're in it for, which is that you want to do your work, and you want to do as good a job as you can, and you want to do it again and again.

BOREL: So you've never fought back against it overtly?

EPHRON: No. To me, living well is the best revenge. You just have to keep writing things and doing what you do. For all of the women who direct, we're always finding ourselves in situations in which people want to take pictures of "women directors." We're always feeling like we're put into a category that is sort of on the side . . .

BOREL: Like you're not real directors—

EPHRON: Exactly. And what all directors do is *exactly* the same thing. You work incredibly long days, you're under unbelievable pressure, you run a movie, which is essentially a small company, for a year at the very minimum. You toss and turn, you take Ambien, you are all the same person. Yet there's this moment when you are suddenly pigeonholed and interviewed every March by some very talented reporter who has just gotten the new statistics that only 13 percent of movies were made by women this year, and how is it possible, and blah blah blah . . . And what you're meant to do in those interviews is complain about how difficult it is. So I don't really like to do those interviews, because to me it's just like, "Write the next movie and try and get it made."

It's always a shock to the people who run studios when

a movie that is for women is a hit. They have an infinite capacity to be shocked. Though I *did* feel that *Bridesmaids* was
some kind of fantastic moment. Aside from the fact that it
was just a hilarious movie, it was great if you wanted to be
political for just a second. It was better than all those movies made by men. It was a huge monster hit, and no huge
movie stars were in it. People *became* stars from having been
in it. I was there opening day at 10:30 in the morning, and I
knew it was going to have a monster weekend. But the studio
didn't know that. Then that was followed by *The Help*. That
was another movie where everyone said, "Who's going to see
that?"

BOREL: Do you think *Bridesmaids* will have a repercussive
effect on the industry?

EPHRON: It will probably be one-eighth of one degree easier
for the next person. But the other great thing about *Bridesmaids* is if anyone still believes that women aren't funny, this
has been the year when you simply would be hooted out of
almost any room for saying that. *Bridesmaids* was like breaking the sound barrier. It was like, "OK, that's that."

IV

SALLY IN HER SIXTIES

BOREL: When you were making *Julie & Julia*, was there a part
of you that related to Julia Child, another pioneering woman
in a field dominated by men?

EPHRON: When I learned to cook and was first exposed to her at the beginning of her career, I don't think in any way I thought, Oh, she and I are similar, but I was interested to realize that her cookbook wasn't published until she was fifty. And I didn't start directing until I was fifty. So that was a way I really felt very connected to her. I certainly felt very connected to that marriage.

BOREL: Because of your marriage to your husband, Nick?

EPHRON: Yes, because I'm so lucky to be with somebody who thinks what I do is great. My sister Delia and I adapted this book for the stage called *Love, Loss, and What I Wore.* There's a part in it that's basically Delia's story of the end of her first marriage. She and her husband were fighting because he didn't want her to write anymore. She had cowritten one book at the time, which was called *The Adventurous Crocheter.* And she sat there during this horrible argument, saying the first sentence of the book over and over in her head: "There is no wrong way to crochet, there are good ways and bad ways but there is no wrong way to crochet . . ." That part really rings a bell for me. When I was in my twenties, I think men had way more serious problems with women working. This was before the women's movement, and that husband of hers was just so threatened by her. And you can barely call that book a success. It's not as though *The Adventurous Crocheter* was a bestseller! He was just threatened because she had done *something.*

BOREL: Nick is a screenwriter, too—do you two use each

other as resources when you're writing? Do you ask Nick for notes; does he ask you for notes?

EPHRON: He doesn't ask me too much, but I'm constantly badgering him to listen to something or read something.

BOREL: Is he good at giving notes?

EPHRON: He's very good, but he's very nice.

BOREL: What do you think Sally would be like if she was sixty-five?

EPHRON: [*Long pause*] Who knows!

BOREL: Do you ever think of the fate of your characters?

EPHRON: Never! Why would you do that? One of the great things about movies is that it's just that short period of time. It's a bubble. The last thing you want to know is that Elizabeth and Darcy had a fight over how to treat the servants!

V
THE MIDAS TOUCH OF COMEDY

BOREL: You've written about hard moments in your life that might have caused another person to hide in bed, or camp out in their therapist's office. How highly do you value that capacity for morphing pain into story?

EPHRON: I think that skill is a good, healthy thing to have. I think my parents taught me and my sisters a truly life-saving technique. "Someday this will be a story!" is a strange thing to say to your weeping child, and it's counterintuitive to me now that I'm a mother, but that's what my parents would say to all of us. [*Pause*] Sometimes I think, Well, we are all really good at it because we're just wildly shallow people. Thank god we learned to do this, because we have no—

BOREL: Soul?

EPHRON: Yes. You said that.

BOREL: Oh, god. I finished your sentence all wrong.

EPHRON: No, it's good! The point is that's who we all are. I don't mean that all four of us are the same person, but we did all get this thing from our parents. And I don't think it was genetic, even though I think almost everything is. You know when they do those studies on identical twins who have been adopted into different families, and then years later you find out that even though they've never met, they both drive a Camaro? Something I've always wondered is if it's the same with sense of humor. I wish they'd do a test on that.

BOREL: Not only do you have a history of making the difficult moments of your life into very funny creative pieces, but also they've turned into some extreme career triumphs for you. *Heartburn*, which was about the dissolution of your marriage, was a wild success, for example. When you were writing it, did you think, I will be vindicated?

EPHRON: No. [*Pause*] I'm going to say something that is not an answer to your question, but it is something I think about. When I did this play called *Imaginary Friends*, about Lillian Hellman and Mary McCarthy, I was very interested to realize that they had both burst out of the crowd by writing things that were shocking. Lillian Hellman wrote *The Children's Hour*, which was about lesbianism. This was in 1930-something and *nobody* ever talked about that. Mary McCarthy wrote something called "The Man in the Brooks Brothers Shirt," which was about having casual sex on a train. That was another thing that nobody wrote about. I realized you could look at the careers of many women writers and see that moment where they did "the shocking thing." If you look at Gloria Steinem and the Playboy Bunny piece, or Joan Didion, who wrote about Hawaii and trying to decide whether to get a divorce or not . . . I could go on and on.

That moment, for me, was not *Heartburn.* It was a piece I wrote in *Esquire* called "A Few Words About Breasts." I knew when I finished writing that piece that it was going to either be a huge success or be judged as a kind of "Who needs to know any of this?" kind of thing. One or the other was going to happen, but I absolutely knew that both were possible. By the time I did *Heartburn*, I was around forty. I had a very clear memory of being at my typewriter in Bridgehampton, where Carl [Bernstein] and I had had a house—that was now in the divorce—but we were still using it at alternate times. I was supposed to be writing a screenplay. And when I started writing, sixteen pages of that novel came out in two days. I thought, Oh, I've found it. The whole time the marriage was breaking up and I was in a state of complete torment and misery, I knew that this would someday be a funny story. I absolutely knew it. It was too horrible. It was too ridiculous not to be.

BOREL: Too horrible to not be interesting.

EPHRON: Yes. You know, even at the time, I was able to not be too horribly victimish about the whole thing. I just don't have that thing. I'm really opposed to it. And I have friends who, four or five years after a divorce, are still complaining about it, or still in court, or still tied in crazy ways to the experience of the end of their marriage. I just have no patience for it at all. I feel terrible for them, but I am very impatient about it. It's like, "Move on, get over it, this is it." You know?

BOREL: There's that great Nietzsche quote: "A joke is an epitaph on the death of a feeling." Making a joke is a good way of removing poison from a moment.

EPHRON: Sure, but it's not the only way. If you look at *The Year of Magical Thinking*, for example, that is *absolutely not* turning a tragic event into anything at all amusing, but instead just turning it into something good.

BOREL: Do you ever find yourself unable to truly feel a moment because you're busy thinking, This will be a story?

EPHRON: Not when things are really bad.

BOREL: But when things are on the verge?

EPHRON: Yes, absolutely. When Carl and I were in the middle of breaking up and we were still together, and he had fallen in love with the wife of the British ambassador, her husband—who was a very, very important political human being—called me. He said, "I think we should get together." And so I said, "Yes. We must." And I asked him where should we get together, and he said, "Someplace out of the way." And I said, "But we're not having the affair! They are!" Anyway, we settled on a Chinese restaurant on Connecticut Avenue. And when we met in front of the restaurant, we fell into each other's arms, weeping. I was pregnant, and it was so horrible, and I said, "Oh, Peter, isn't it awful?" He said, "Yes, it's just awful . . . What's happening to *this country?*" And you know, I didn't stop crying, but I thought, Oh, that is hilarious. I knew someday I could use that. And it's in *Heartburn!* The point is: It doesn't mean I wasn't a complete basket case, but if you are a writer that is what you do. That's what your life is for, to feed the animal.

BOREL: Does it make you greedy for those moments, do you think?

EPHRON: I think it makes some people greedy for those moments. Tom Wolfe once said this really brilliant thing. This was about thirty years ago. He was giving a speech about reporting, and how important it is for a writer to keep reporting, and to be able to get outside their self. He said that "some fiction writers"—and he was clearly referring to Philip Roth—are like Charles Lamb's essay on a roast pig, which is that they think they have to burn the house down to cook the pig. What he was talking about was Philip Roth going through one woman after another, and writing one book after another about them. You cannot in any way—thirty years later—say that Tom Wolfe was right about Philip Roth, because his body of work is just too fantastic. But he is someone who, if he gets cancer, he puts it in the next book. I think for some people it's a very short distance between it happening and it becoming a book. I think some people probably create a certain amount of uproar in their lives in order to have the next thing to write about. But I don't think I ever did that.

NORA EPHRON was born in Manhattan in 1941 and grew up in Beverly Hills. Her parents were Broadway playwrights, who would base the play *Take Her, She's Mine* on letters she sent home from Wellesley College. After graduation, Ephron became a journalist, writing for the *New York Post*, *New York* magazine, *The New York Times Sunday Magazine*, *Cosmopolitan*, and *Esquire*, where her 1972 piece "A Few Words About Breasts" made her a household name as an essayist. Her marriage to and subsequent divorce from Watergate reporter Carl Bernstein inspired her first novel, *Heartburn*, which was published in 1983 and later became a movie starring Meryl Streep and Jack Nicholson. She was nominated for an Academy Award for Best Writing for the films *Silkwood*, *When Harry Met Sally . . .* , and *Sleepless in Seattle*, and her essay collection *I Feel Bad About My Neck* was a number-one *New York Times* bestseller. She died in New York City in 2012, at the age of seventy-one.

MICHAEL S. LASKY is an award-winning journalist and the author of two books and hundreds of articles for national magazines and newspapers. He was formerly a magazine editor for more than twenty years.

PATRICK McGILLIGAN is the author of *Fritz Lang: The Nature of the Beast* and *George Cukor: A Double Life*—both *New York Times* Notable Books—and the Edgar Award–nominated

Alfred Hitchcock: A Life in Darkness and Light. His many film books include the *Backstory* series of interviews with screenwriters, which includes, in volume five, Nora Ephron.

KERRY LAUERMAN is a senior editor at *The Washington Post.*

KATHRYN BOREL is the author of the book *Corked: A Memoir,* and currently writes for the animated comedy series *American Dad!* She is also the interviews editor at *The Believer* magazine.

THE LAST INTERVIEW SERIES

KURT VONNEGUT: THE LAST INTERVIEW

"I think it can be tremendously refreshing if a creator of literature has something on his mind other than the history of literature so far. Literature should not disappear up its own asshole, so to speak."

$15.95 / $17.95 CAN
978-1-61219-090-7
ebook: 978-1-61219-091-4

LEARNING TO LIVE FINALLY: THE LAST INTERVIEW
JACQUES DERRIDA

"I am at war with myself, it's true, you couldn't possibly know to what extent ... I say contradictory things that are, we might say, in real tension; they are what construct me, make me live, and will make me die."

translated by PASCAL-ANNE BRAULT and MICHAEL NAAS

$15.95 / $17.95 CAN
978-1-61219-094-5
ebook: 978-1-61219-032-7

ROBERTO BOLAÑO: THE LAST INTERVIEW

"Posthumous: It sounds like the name of a Roman gladiator, an unconquered gladiator. At least that's what poor Posthumous would like to believe. It gives him courage."

translated by SYBIL PEREZ and others

$15.95 / $17.95 CAN
978-1-61219-095-2
ebook: 978-1-61219-033-4

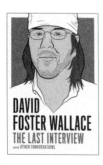

DAVID FOSTER WALLACE: THE LAST INTERVIEW

"I don't know what you're thinking or what it's like inside you and you don't know what it's like inside me. In fiction ... we can leap over that wall itself in a certain way."

$15.95 / $15.95 CAN
978-1-61219-206-2
ebook: 978-1-61219-207-9

THE LAST INTERVIEW SERIES

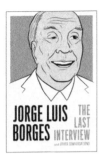

JORGE LUIS BORGES: THE LAST INTERVIEW

"Believe me: the benefits of blindness have been greatly exaggerated. If I could see, I would never leave the house, I'd stay indoors reading the many books that surround me."

translated by KIT MAUDE

$15.95 / $15.95 CAN
978-1-61219-204-8
ebook: 978-1-61219-205-5

HANNAH ARENDT: THE LAST INTERVIEW

"There are no dangerous thoughts for the simple reason that thinking itself is such a dangerous enterprise."

$15.95 / $15.95 CAN
978-1-61219-311-3
ebook: 978-1-61219-312-0

RAY BRADBURY: THE LAST INTERVIEW

"You don't have to destroy books to destroy a culture. Just get people to stop reading them."

$15.95 / $15.95 CAN
978-1-61219-421-9
ebook: 978-1-61219-422-6

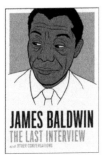

JAMES BALDWIN: THE LAST INTERVIEW

"You don't realize that you're intelligent until it gets you into trouble."

$15.95 / $15.95 CAN
978-1-61219-400-4
ebook: 978-1-61219-401-1

THE LAST INTERVIEW SERIES

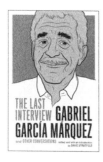

GABRIEL GÁRCIA MÁRQUEZ: THE LAST INTERVIEW

"The only thing the Nobel Prize is good for is not having to wait in line."

$15.95 / $15.95 CAN
978-1-61219-480-6
ebook: 978-1-61219-481-3

LOU REED: THE LAST INTERVIEW

"Hubert Selby. William Burroughs. Allen Ginsberg. Delmore Schwartz . . . I thought if you could do what those writers did and put it to drums and guitar, you'd have the greatest thing on earth."

$15.95 / $15.95 CAN
978-1-61219-478-3
ebook: 978-1-61219-479-0